Language Learning Stations Grades 6–8

English Language Arts series

Authors: Schyrlet Cameron and Suzanne Myers
Editors: Mary Dieterich and Sarah M. Anderson
Proofreader: Margaret Brown

COPYRIGHT © 2013 Mark Twain Media, Inc.

ISBN 978-1-62223-001-3

Printing No. CD-404179

Mark Twain Media, Inc., Publishers
Distributed by Carson-Dellosa Publishing LLC

The purchase of this book entitles the buyer to reproduce the student pages for classroom use only. Other permissions may be obtained by writing Mark Twain Media, Inc., Publishers.

All rights reserved. Printed in the United States of America.

Visit us at www.carsondellosa.com

Table of Contents

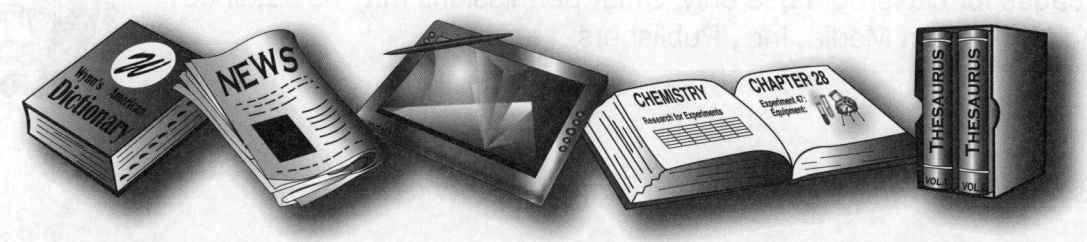

To the Teacher 1
Common Core State Standards Matrix 2

Unit: Punctuation Usage
Teacher Page 3
Activities
Station One: *The Comma: Nonrestrictive Elements* 4
Station Two: *The Dash* 5
Station Three: *Parentheses* 6
Station Four: *Coordinate Adjectives* 7

Unit: Spelling Conventions
Teacher Page 8
Activities
Station One: *Using Spelling Rules* 9
Station Two: *Homonyms* 10
Station Three: *Confusing Word Pairs* 11
Station Four: *Syllables* 12
Station Five: *Commonly Misspelled Words* 13
Reflection: *Spelling Conventions* 14
Handouts
Spelling Rules 15
150 Commonly Misspelled Words 16

Unit: Reference Materials
Teacher Page 17
Activities
Station One: *Syllabication* 18
Station Two: *Pronunciation of a Word* 19
Station Three: *Parts of Speech* 20
Station Four: *The Word Meaning Game* ... 21
Station Five: *Thesaurus* 22
Station Six: *Glossary* 23

Unit: Roots and Affixes
Teacher Page 24
Activities
Station One: *Root Words* 25
Station Two: *Adding Affixes* 26
Station Three: *Root Words, Affixes, and Context Clues* 27
Station Four: *Plural Forms of Latin Nouns* 28
Handouts
Prefixes and Suffixes 29
Greek and Latin Roots 30
Pollyanna 31

Unit: Figurative Language
Teacher Page 32
Activities
Station One: *Alliteration* 33
Station Two: *Metaphors in Newspapers* 34
Station Three: *Figurative Language in Advertisements* 35
Station Four: *Idioms* 36
Handout
Figures of Speech 37

Unit: Vocabulary and Word Choice
Teacher Page 38
Activities
Station One: *Mood* 39
Station Two: *Word Choice* 40
Station Three: *Connotations: Positive, Negative, or Neutral* 41
Station Four: *Vocabulary* 42
Handout
"The Star-Spangled Banner" 43

Answer Keys 44

To the Teacher

In the *English Language Arts* (ELA) *series*, students in grades six through eight explore reading, writing, and language in a learning station environment. Learning stations engage students in individual or small group activities. Learning stations are an instructional strategy that can be used to target specific skills.

Each book in the ELA series features five or six units of study. Each unit has a teacher page that identifies the goal, states the standards, lists materials and setup for the activities, and provides instructions to be presented to students. Also, there are questions for opening discussion and student reflection. (Note: It is important for the teacher to introduce, model, or review the concepts or skills with the students at the beginning of each unit.)

Books in the ELA Series

- *Reading: Literature Learning Stations, Grades 6–8*
  The units focus on alliteration, rhyme, plot and setting, tone and mood, and poetry.

- *Reading: Informational Text Learning Stations, Grades 6–8*
  The units focus on citing evidence, bias, point of view, propaganda techniques, organizational text structures, and text features.

- *Writing Learning Stations, Grades 6–8*
  The units focus on fact and opinion, characterization, making inferences, proofreading, and dialogue.

- *Language Learning Stations, Grades 6–8*
  The units focus on punctuation, dictionary usage, figurative language, roots and affixes, and word meaning.

Language Learning Stations, Grades 6–8, contains six units of study. Each unit consists of four to six learning station activities. The activity at each station is designed to create interest, provide practice, and stimulate discussion. These units will help students become better readers as they learn to cite evidence from the text and become aware of spelling rules and conventions; punctuation; root words, suffixes and prefixes; and figurative language. Whenever applicable, media/technology and speaking/listening skills are integrated into the activity. Handouts are provided as supplemental resources.

The units of study in the ELA series are meant to supplement or enhance the regular classroom English Language Arts curriculum. The station activities are correlated to the strands of the English Language Arts Common Core State Standards.

Common Core State Standards Matrix

English Language Arts Standards: Language

Units of Study	Grade Level																
	L.6.1	L.6.2	L.6.3	L.6.4	L.6.5	L.6.6	L.7.1	L.7.2	L.7.3	L.7.4	L.7.5	L.7.6	L.8.1	L.8.2	L.8.3	L.8.4	L.8.5	L.8.6
Punctuation Usage		X						X						X				
Spelling Conventions		X						X						X				
Reference Materials				X						X						X		
Roots and Affixes				X						X						X		
Figurative Language					X						X						X	
Vocabulary and Word Choice						X						X						X

© Copyright 2010. National Governors Association Center for Best Practices and Council of Chief State School Officers. All rights reserved.

Teacher Page

Unit: Punctuation Usage

Goal: Students will be able to correctly use commas, parentheses, and dashes to set off nonrestrictive/parenthetical elements. Students will also be able to use a comma to separate coordinate adjectives.

Common Core State Standards (CCSS):

6th Grade	7th Grade	8th Grade
L.6.2a. Use punctuation (commas, parentheses, dashes) to set off nonrestrictive/parenthetical elements.	L.7.2a. Use a comma to separate coordinate adjectives (e.g., *It was a fascinating, enjoyable movie* but not *He wore an old [,] green shirt.*).	L.8.2a. Use punctuation (comma, ellipsis, dash) to indicate a pause or break

© Copyright 2010. National Governors Association Center for Best Practices and Council of Chief State School Officers. All rights reserved.

Materials List/Setup

Station 1: The Comma: Nonrestrictive Elements (Activity)
Station 2: The Dash (Activity)
Station 3: Parentheses (Activity)
Station 4: Coordinate Adjectives (Activity)

Activity: one copy per student

Opening: Discussion Questions (Teacher-Directed)

1. Do you find it difficult to know when to use a comma? How about a dash or parentheses?
2. What are nonrestrictive elements?
3. What are coordinate adjectives?

Student Instructions for Learning Stations

At the learning stations, you will practice punctuating sentences containing nonrestrictive/parenthetical elements and coordinate adjectives. Discuss your answers with other team members after completing each activity.

Closure: Reflection

1. When would you use parentheses instead of a comma?
2. Which type of punctuation (commas, dashes, or parentheses) do you see most often used in literature?

Language Learning Stations — Punctuation Usage

Name: _____ Date: _____

Station One: The Comma: Nonrestrictive Elements

A **nonrestrictive element** is a word, a group of words, or a clause that is added to a sentence to give more information, but it could be removed from the sentence without changing the meaning. Most nonrestrictive elements are set off by commas.

> **Example** (Nonrestrictive): That dress, **which has a ruffle around the bottom**, won a first-place ribbon at the county fair.

Directions: Insert commas to set off the nonrestrictive elements.

1. Rhode Island the smallest state in land area is a great place to go on vacation.

2. The rose bush in the front yard which I planted needs to be trimmed.

3. The Washington Monument built between 1848 and 1884 was damaged by an earthquake.

4. The candidate who has a degree in speech communication was able to keep his speech under the thirty-minute time limit.

5. Mr. Jones who likes to play golf is a candidate for mayor.

6. My youngest brother who lives in Oregon helped me design a website for my company.

7. Teresa the friendliest girl in our class was elected student body president.

8. The *Mona Lisa* painted by Leonardo da Vinci hangs in the Louvre Museum.

9. Michael the oldest child in our family was named after our uncle.

10. John Philip Sousa an American composer was famous for his patriotic marches.

Language Learning Stations | Punctuation Usage

Name: _____ Date: _____

Station Two: The Dash

Rules for Using Dashes

A **dash** can be used to indicate:
a. an abrupt termination of a sentence.
b. a faltering or hesitating speech.
c. a sudden unexpected interruption in thought or speech.
d. a longer than normal pause or break.

Directions: Read the following excerpts from *The Voyages of Dr. Dolittle* by Hugh Lofting. Determine which rule was followed in using the dash. Place the letter of the rule on the blank beside each excerpt.

_____ 1. We find their shells in the rocks—turned to stone—thousands of years old.

_____ 2. Then one of them, the leader—a little man—stood up and turned to the judge.

_____ 3. "I was, Doctor," said Bob, "and I tell you—"

_____ 4. "Ah—at last!" said the Doctor. "Good old Dab-Dab!"

_____ 5. But it's—er—a little hard to make any one exactly understand the situation.

_____ 6. Then the fireplace—the biggest fireplace you ever saw—was like a room in itself.

_____ 7. "I protest, I object!" screamed the prosecutor. "Your Honor, this is—"

_____ 8. The study of plants—or botany, as it is called—was a kind of natural history which had never interested me very much.

_____ 9. "Well—" she thought a moment— "I really don't see why not."

_____ 10. "That's a good idea—splendid—if he'll come."

CD-404179 ©Mark Twain Media, Inc., Publishers

LANGUAGE LEARNING STATIONS Punctuation Usage

Name: _____ Date: _____

Station Three: Parentheses

Parentheses are used in sentences to enclose nonrestrictive elements that explain the preceding word or phrase. Unlike commas or dashes, parentheses are always used in pairs ( ).

Example: Felines (lions, tigers, cheetahs, and leopards) are meat-eaters.

Directions: The following are excerpts from *The Voyages of Doctor Dolittle* by Hugh Lofting. Rewrite each sentence and insert parentheses where needed.

1. Green lizards which were very rare in Puddleby sat up on the stones in the sunlight and blinked at us.

2. After swooping over the sea around me just looking for food, I supposed, he went off in the direction from which he had come.

3. I and my sister, Clippa she was my favorite sister, had a very narrow escape for our lives.

4. He kept getting out his sextant an instrument which tells you what part of the ocean you are in and making calculations.

5. "The Sea!" murmured poor Clippa with a faraway look in her eyes she had fine eyes, had my sister, Clippa.

Station Four: Coordinate Adjectives

Coordinate adjectives are a series of adjectives that separately describe the noun and are equal in importance. A comma should be placed between the adjectives.

> **Coordinate Adjectives**
>
> There are two tests you can apply to determine if the adjectives are coordinating. Both tests must work, or the adjectives are not coordinates.
>
> **Coordinate Adjectives: Levy is a kind, selfless teenager.**
>
> 1. If you insert the word "and" between the adjectives, does the sentence still make sense?
>   Example: Levy is a kind **and** selfless teenager.
>
> 2. If you reverse the order of the adjectives, does the sentence still make sense?
>   Example: Levy is a **selfless, kind** teenager.

Directions: If the underlined adjectives are coordinates, insert a comma between the adjectives. Not all sentences will contain coordinate adjectives.

1. The <u>light fluffy</u> mousse was a perfect dessert for the luncheon.

2. We were prepared for a <u>long tedious</u> wait in the emergency room.

3. My bedroom walls were painted with a <u>light green</u> paint.

4. The <u>mouth-watering delicious</u> cake was served at her birthday party.

5. The scenic route is a <u>narrow winding</u> road that leads up to the mountains.

6. Susie had a <u>juicy ripe</u> apple for her mid-morning snack.

7. Tina was a <u>beautiful ballet</u> dancer.

8. The chef prepared <u>flaky moist</u> fish for his customers.

9. The spectators watched a <u>long grueling</u> football game.

10. Flora fell on the <u>slippery wet</u> sidewalk.

LANGUAGE LEARNING STATIONS | Spelling Conventions

Teacher Page

Unit: Spelling Conventions

Goal: Students will be able to apply spelling rules in order to spell correctly when writing.

Common Core State Standards (CCSS):

6th Grade	7th Grade	8th Grade
L.6.2. Demonstrate command of the conventions of standard English capitalization, punctuation, and spelling when writing. b. Spell correctly.	L.7.2. Demonstrate command of the conventions of standard English capitalization, punctuation, and spelling when writing. b. Spell correctly.	L.8.2. Demonstrate command of the conventions of standard English capitalization, punctuation, and spelling when writing. b. Spell correctly.

© Copyright 2010. National Governors Association Center for Best Practices and Council of Chief State School Officers. All rights reserved.

Materials List/Setup

Station 1: Using Spelling Rules (Activity); Spelling Rules (Handout)
Station 2: Homonyms (Activity)
Station 3: Confusing Word Pairs (Activity)
Station 4: Syllables (Activity); print or online dictionaries
Station 5: Commonly Misspelled Words (Activity); Commonly Misspelled Word List (Handout); Dictionaries (print or online); sandpaper; colored pens

Activity: one copy per student
Handout: one copy per each student in a group

*Integration of Technology Skills and Speaking and Listening Standards

Opening: Discussion Questions (Teacher-Directed)

1. Which word is the most difficult for you to remember how to spell?
2. Do you know any spelling rules?

Student Instructions for Learning Stations

At the learning stations, you will apply your knowledge of spelling skills. Discuss your answers with other team members after completing each activity.

Closure: Reflection

Students will use the completed learning station activities to help compose the Reflection: Spelling Conventions activity.

Language Learning Stations | Spelling Conventions

Name: _____ Date: _____

Station One: Using Spelling Rules

Directions: One of the words in column one is spelled incorrectly. Write the correctly spelled word in column two. Write the spelling rule(s) that helped you decide which word was spelled correctly. Use the Spelling Rules handout if you need help.

Word Pairs	Correct Spelling	Rule
1. conscience/consceince		
2. accelerator/accelerater		
3. acqire/acquire		
4. torpedos/torpedoes		
5. weight/wieght		
6. unnecessary/uneccessary		
7. shamful/shameful		
8. referring/refering		
9. elfes/elves		
10. suppression/suppresstion		

CD-404179 ©Mark Twain Media, Inc., Publishers

Language Learning Stations — Spelling Conventions

Name: _____ Date: _____

Station Two: Homonyms

Homonyms are two or more words that are spelled alike, pronounced alike, or both, but the words have different meanings.

Example: *(same pronunciation, different spelling)* plain, plane
Example: *(same spelling, different pronunciation)* object, object
Example: *(same spelling and pronunciation)* fair, fair

Directions: Read the definitions for the word pairs. Write a sentence using one of the words from the pair.

Word Pairs	Sentence
accept: to take in except: other than	
aid: to assist aide: one who gives assistance	
aisle: a passageway isle: an island	
altar: a table in a church alter: to change	
capital: a chief city capitol: a building where the legislature meets	
tear: to rip tear: watery fluid from the eye	
passed: went by; left behind past: a previous time	
principal: the head of a school principle: a rule or belief	
their: shows ownership they're: a contraction for "they are"	
waist: the mid-section of the body waste: to wear away; garbage	

Language Learning Stations | Spelling Conventions

Name: _____ Date: _____

Station Three: Confusing Word Pairs

Directions: Read the definitions for each of the confusing word pairs. Then write a sentence for each word.

already: previously; by this time
all ready: completely prepared

1. already: _____
   _____

2. all ready: _____
   _____

altogether: entirely; wholly
all together: people or things gathered in one place

3. altogether: _____
   _____

4. all together: _____
   _____

affect: influence
effect: result; to cause

5. affect: _____
   _____

6. effect: _____
   _____

angel: refers to a heavenly being
angle: shape made by the meeting of two lines; to scheme or use tricks to get something

7. angel: _____
   _____

8. angle: _____
   _____

Language Learning Stations | Spelling Conventions

Name: _____ Date: _____

Station Four: Syllables

Syllables are the individual sounds that make up a word. Breaking a word into syllables makes it easier to remember the correct spelling of the word. **Example:** per/cen/tile

Directions: Read each word below and clap your hands once for each syllable you hear. In the second column, write the word using a slash mark (/) between each syllable you heard. In the third column, show how a dictionary divides the word.

Word Pairs	Divide Into Syllables (/) by Clapping	Divide Into Syllables (/) Using a Dictionary
1. revolution		
2. capital		
3. bandit		
4. man		
5. rubber		
6. declaration		
7. pencil		
8. preamble		
9. unsuspected		
10. important		
11. elect		
12. athlete		
13. twilight		
14. umpire		
15. paddle		
16. vacant		
17. blank		
18. calculate		
19. temper		
20. chip		

CD-404179 ©Mark Twain Media, Inc., Publishers

Language Learning Stations | Spelling Conventions

Name: _____ Date: _____

Station Five: Commonly Misspelled Words

From the Commonly Misspelled Words list, select ten words that you have trouble spelling correctly. Write those words below.

1. _____
2. _____
3. _____
4. _____
5. _____
6. _____
7. _____
8. _____
9. _____
10. _____

Divide each of your words into syllables.

1. _____
2. _____
3. _____
4. _____
5. _____
6. _____
7. _____
8. _____
9. _____
10. _____

Write the words using a different colored pen for each word.

1. _____
2. _____
3. _____
4. _____
5. _____
6. _____
7. _____
8. _____
9. _____
10. _____

Using your finger, write each word on a piece of sandpaper.

Finally, have another group member give you a spelling test over your ten words.

How many did you get right? _____

Language Learning Stations — Spelling Conventions

Name: _____ Date: _____

Reflection: Spelling Conventions

What are five things you could do to strengthen your skills in spelling?

_____
_____
_____
_____
_____
_____
_____
_____
_____
_____

Why is it important to proofread your work?

_____
_____
_____
_____
_____
_____
_____
_____
_____
_____
_____
_____

Spelling Rules

Below is a list of some of the most common spelling rules. Learning these rules will help you to become a better speller. Remember, there are many exceptions to the spelling rules. Use a dictionary when you are unsure about the spelling of a word.

Rule	Example
Many words end in the **er** sound. It can be spelled **er**, **or**, and **ar**. Most words end with the **er** spelling.	avenger, creator, regular
Use **y**, **ey**, or **ie** to make the **long e** sound at the end of words.	country, money, baggie
Q is almost always followed by **u**.	quite, queen, quarry
The spelling **ce** is used for words with a long vowel sound followed by the ending **s** sound.	ice, device, space
se or **ce** can be used for short vowel words ending in the **s** sound.	service, notice, dense
Write **i** before **e** when the vowel sound is **long e** except after **c**.	believe, relief, deceive
Write **e** before **i** when the vowel sound is **long a**.	weigh, freight, reign
Plurals • Add **s** to most nouns and verbs • Add **es** if words end in **ch**, **sh**, **x**, **s**, or **z**. • Change the **y** to an **i** and add **es** if a word ending in **y** is preceded by a consonant • Add **es** to most words that end in the letter **o**. If the letter **o** is preceded by a vowel, just add an **s**. • For words that end in **f** or **fe**, change the **f** or **fe** to **v** and add **es**.	cats, states, runs churches, rushes, boxes, buses, buzzes parties, tries, replies echoes, potatoes, rodeos shelves, wives, knives
Adding a prefix never changes the spelling of a word.	dislike, indoors, misspell
Adding Suffixes • In most cases, don't change the spelling, just add the suffix. • In most cases, drop the silent **e** at the end, if the suffix begins with a vowel (-able, -ing, -ed). • In most cases, words ending in silent **e** keep the **e** if the suffix begins with a consonant (-ly, -ful, -less). • Double the final consonant if the word has one syllable or the suffix begins with a vowel (-ing, -ed).	walker, walking, walked saving, lovable, raced safely, hopeless, hopeful sitting, napped, running
Use the full spelling of both words for compound words.	moonlight, outdoor, into
To spell the **shun** sound at the ends of words • use **ion** or **sion** when the root word ends in **s** or **d**. • use **cian** for root words that have to do with people. • use **tion** for everything else.	expression, suspension physician, musician station, ration, celebration
Most of the time, adjectives use the **ary** ending, and nouns use the **ery** ending.	revolutionary, battery, stationary, stationery

150 Commonly Misspelled Words

a lot	environment	lightning	pronunciation
acceptable	everyone	loneliness	questionnaire
accidentally	everything	losing	receipt
accommodate	exceed	maintenance	receive
acquaintance	existence	maneuver	recommend
acquire	experience	mathematics	reference
again	experiment	medieval	relevant
all right	favorite	memento	responsible
always	fiery	millimeter	restaurant
amateur	finally	miniature	rhythm
anxious	foreign	minuscule	ridiculous
anyone	forty	mischievous	schedules
apparent	friend	misspell	scissors
argument	gauge	neighbor	secretary
average	government	no one	separate
beautiful	grateful	noticeable	shepherd
because	guarantee	nuisance	sincerely
before	guess	occasionally	souvenir
believe	happened	occurrence	supersede
brought	happily	opportunity	temperature
calendar	harass	outrageous	thought
campaign	heard	pamphlet	through
canceled	height	parallel	tongue
category	immediate	pastime	tonight
caught	independent	perceive	truly
cemetery	indispensable	perseverance	twelfth
changeable	inoculate	personnel	unanimous
collectible	instead	playwright	until
column	intelligence	possess	usually
committed	interrupt	potato	vacuum
committee	jealousy	precede	valuable
definitely	jewelry	preferred	visible
different	judgment	prejudice	weather
disappear	leisure	principal	Wednesday
discipline	length	principle	whether
eighth	liaison	privilege	zoology
eligible	library	probably	
embarrass	license	procedure	

LANGUAGE LEARNING STATIONS | Reference Materials

Teacher Page

Unit: Reference Materials

Goal: Students will be able to locate and use information found in a dictionary, thesaurus, and glossary.

Common Core State Standards (CCSS):

6th Grade	7th Grade	8th Grade
L.6.4. Determine or clarify the meaning of unknown and multiple-meaning words and phrases based on grade 6 reading and content, choosing flexibly from a range of strategies. c. Consult reference materials (e.g., dictionaries, glossaries, thesauruses), both print and digital, to find the pronunciation of a word or determine or clarify its precise meaning or its part of speech.	L.7.4. Determine or clarify the meaning of unknown and multiple-meaning words and phrases based on grade 7 reading and content, choosing flexibly from a range of strategies. c. Consult general and specialized reference materials (e.g., dictionaries, glossaries, thesauruses), both print and digital, to find the pronunciation of a word or determine or clarify its precise meaning or its part of speech.	L.8.4. Determine or clarify the meaning of unknown and multiple-meaning words and phrases based on grade 8 reading and content, choosing flexibly from a range of strategies. c. Consult general and specialized reference materials (e.g., dictionaries, glossaries, thesauruses), both print and digital, to find the pronunciation of a word or determine or clarify its precise meaning or its part of speech.

© Copyright 2010. National Governors Association Center for Best Practices and Council of Chief State School Officers. All rights reserved.

Materials List/Setup

Station 1: Syllabication (Activity); dictionaries (print or online)
Station 2: Pronunciation of a Word (Activity); dictionaries (print or online)
Station 3: Parts of Speech (Activity); dictionaries (print or online)
Station 4: Word Meaning (Activity); dictionaries (print or online)
Station 5: Thesaurus (Activity); thesaurus (print or online)
Station 6: Glossary (Activity); textbooks (must contain a glossary); dictionaries (print)

Activity: one copy per student
Dictionaries: one copy per each student in a group

*Integration of Technology Skills—Online Dictionary and Thesaurus: <http://www.merriam-webster.com/>

Opening Activity and Discussion Questions (Teacher-Directed)

1. Do you have a dictionary or thesaurus at home?
2. Which do you use more often: a print or online dictionary?
3. Do you find yourself using the same words over and over again in your writing?

Student Instructions for Learning Stations

At the learning stations, you will use a dictionary, thesaurus, or glossary to locate information. Discuss your answers with other team members after completing each activity.

Closure: Reflection

The following questions can be used to stimulate discussion or as a journaling activity.
1. Why do most social studies textbooks contain a glossary?
2. What is the difference between a thesaurus and a dictionary?

LANGUAGE LEARNING STATIONS   Reference Materials

Name: _____ Date: _____

Station One: Syllabication

A **syllable** consists of a word or word part. Each syllable has one vowel sound. Syllables can be used to help with the pronunciation of words.

Syllabication Rules
1. Divide between two middle consonants, (ap/pear, cot/ton, num/ber). [Exception: do not divide consonant digraphs, such as **ch**, **gh**, **kn**, **ph**, **sh**, **th**, etc.]
2. Divide before a single middle consonant (me/ter, pu/pil, wa/ter).
3. Divide between root words in compound words (out/door, stair/way, class/room).
4. Divide root words from prefixes and suffixes that have a vowel sound (a/bate/ment, com/pile, noise/less).
5. Divide before the consonant if the consonant is followed by "**-le**" at the end of the word (i/ci/cle, mus/cle, as/sem/ble).

Directions Use the above rules to divide the words below into syllables. Then list the number of the rule used to divide the word. Some words may require more than one rule to divide it into syllables. Use a print or online dictionary if you need help.

Word	Word Divided Into Syllables (/)	Number of the Rule(s)
1. hallway		
2. dessert		
3. eager		
4. keyboard		
5. pinnacle		
6. program		
7. quickly		
8. responsible		
9. repel		
10. starkness		

CD-404179 ©Mark Twain Media, Inc., Publishers

| Language Learning Stations | Reference Materials |

Name: _____ Date: _____

Station Two: Pronunciation of a Word

In a dictionary, the **pronunciation** of a word will usually come immediately after the main entry word. A pronunciation key will usually be found at the front or back of a dictionary. A pronunciation key is a guide to help you pronounce the word. It displays symbols with examples of words that have the same sound as each symbol. Accent marks are used to show which syllable is to be stressed.

Directions: Try to pronounce each word below. Use the pronunciation key located in a dictionary if you need help. Write the correct spelling of the word on the line beside the pronunciation. Use a dictionary to verify your answers.

1. läj _____
2. kwilt _____
3. hôr′ ər _____
4. tel′ ə fōn′ _____
5. kə lek′ shən _____
6. ôr′ ə jin _____
7. kän′ dukt _____
8. brouz _____
9. swä′ lō _____
10. nā′ chər _____
11. pan′ ik _____
12. hab′ it _____
13. lit′ ər ə chər _____
14. ā′ kər _____
15. käl′ ij _____

Language Learning Stations — Reference Materials

Name: _____ Date: _____

Station Three: Parts of Speech

Many words have multiple meanings. The way the word is used in a sentence determines its part of speech. A dictionary can help you identify the parts of speech for words.

Parts of Speech	
adj.	adjective
adv.	adverb
conj.	conjunction
interj.	interjection
n.	noun
prep.	preposition
pron.	pronoun

Directions: Write a sentence for each word. On the short blank beside each word identify the part of speech for the word as it is used in the sentence. Use a dictionary to check your work.

1. conduct _____

   _____

   _____

2. grade _____

   _____

   _____

3. produce _____

   _____

   _____

4. ruin _____

   _____

   _____

5. transport _____

   _____

   _____

Language Learning Stations · Reference Materials

Name: _____ Date: _____

Station Four: The Word Meaning Game

Directions: Browse a dictionary for unfamiliar or obscure words. Select three words to use for the game below, and write each word on a blank. Write either the real definition of the word and its correct usage in a sentence, or write a pretend definition for the word and a sentence that works with its pretend meaning.

1. Word: _____

   Definition: _____

   Sentence: _____
   _____

2. Word: _____

   Definition: _____

   Sentence: _____
   _____

3. Word: _____

   Definition: _____

   Sentence: _____
   _____

How To Play The Word Meaning Game

Select one of the words from your completed list. Read the word, definition, and sentence to other students in your group. Each person in the group will make a guess as to whether you are giving a real or pretend usage of the word. If a player is correct, he or she receives two points, and you receive zero points. If someone answers incorrectly, you receive two points. The game continues with players taking turns with words on their lists. The person with the most points wins the game!

LANGUAGE LEARNING STATIONS

Reference Materials

Name: _____ Date: _____

Station Five: Thesaurus

A **synonym** is a word that has the same or almost the same meaning as another word. A **thesaurus** is a book of synonyms. Thesauruses are usually arranged by lists of words grouped together by similar meanings or in alphabetical order by entry words.

Directions: The words below can be used as nouns or verbs. Look up each word in a thesaurus. Find a synonym that is a noun and a synonym that is a verb for each word. Write the synonyms in the appropriate column.

Word	Noun	Verb
1. cook	_____	_____
2. finish	_____	_____
3. shelter	_____	_____
4. present	_____	_____
5. judge	_____	_____
6. broadcast	_____	_____
7. awareness	_____	_____
8. change	_____	_____
9. curl	_____	_____
10. beam	_____	_____
11. flood	_____	_____
12. guide	_____	_____
13. transport	_____	_____
14. supply	_____	_____
15. process	_____	_____

Name: ______________________ Date: ______________________

Station Six: Glossary

A **glossary**, which is a mini-dictionary, is found at the back of a book. A glossary usually only has words found in that book. The amount of information provided in a glossary will vary.

Directions: Look up a word in the glossary of a textbook. Now look up the same word in a dictionary. Compare and contrast the types of information found in each.

Word: ______________

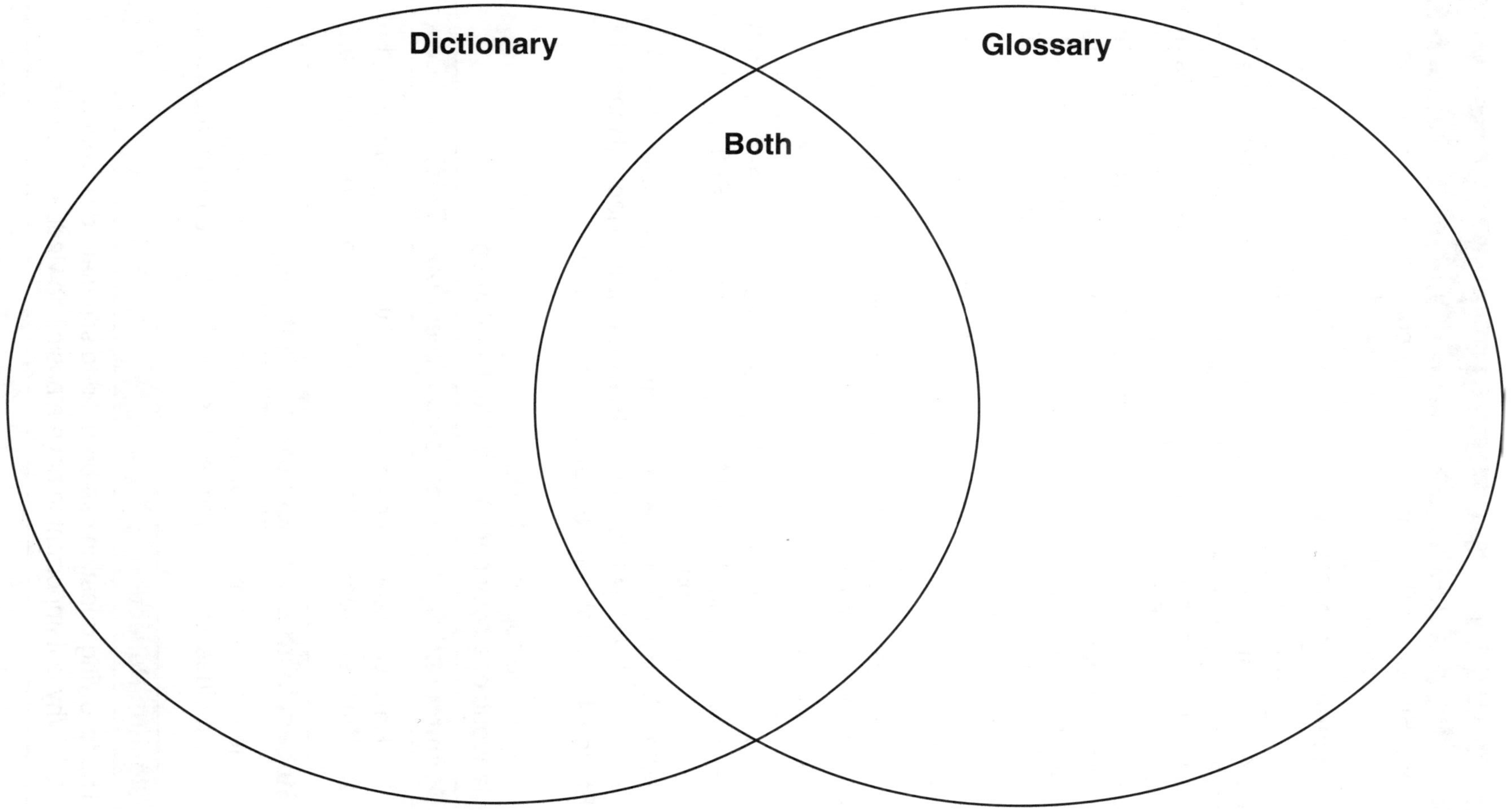

| Language Learning Stations | Roots and Affixes |

Teacher Page

Unit: Roots and Affixes

Goal: Students will be able to identify common root words, including Greek or Latin roots, and affixes to determine the meaning of a word.

Common Core State Standards (CCSS):

6th Grade	7th Grade	8th Grade
L.6.4. Determine or clarify the meaning of unknown and multiple-meaning words and phrases based on grade 6 reading and content, choosing flexibly from a range of strategies. b. Use common, grade-appropriate Greek or Latin affixes and roots as clues to the meaning of a word (e.g., audience, auditory, audible).	L.7.4. Determine or clarify the meaning of unknown and multiple-meaning words and phrases based on grade 7 reading and content, choosing flexibly from a range of strategies. b. Use common, grade-appropriate Greek or Latin affixes and roots as clues to the meaning of a word (e.g., belligerent, bellicose, rebel).	L.8.4. Determine or clarify the meaning of unknown and multiple-meaning words and phrases based on grade 8 reading and content, choosing flexibly from a range of strategies. b. Use common, grade-appropriate Greek or Latin affixes and roots as clues to the meaning of a word (e.g., precede, recede, secede).

© Copyright 2010. National Governors Association Center for Best Practices and Council of Chief State School Officers. All rights reserved.

Materials List/Setup

Station 1:   Root Words (Activity); Prefixes and Suffixes (Handout)
Station 2:   Adding Affixes (Activity); Prefixes and Suffixes (Handout); Greek and Latin Roots (Handout)
Station 3:   Root Words, Affixes, and Context Clues (Activity); *Pollyanna* (Handout); Prefixes and Suffixes (Handout); Greek and Latin Roots (Handout)
Station 4:   Plural Form of Latin Nouns (Activity)

Activity: one copy per student
Handout: one copy per each student in a group

Opening Activity and Discussion Questions (Teacher-Directed)

1. Have you ever come across a word you could pronounce, but you didn't know its meaning?
2. What are some clues that can help you figure out the meaning of an unfamiliar word?

Student Instructions for Learning Stations

At the learning stations, you will determine the meaning of words using root words, affixes, and context clues. Discuss your answers with other team members after completing each activity.

Closure: Reflection

The following question can be used to stimulate discussion or as a journaling activity.
1. Why is it important to have a basic knowledge of affixes?

| Language Learning Stations | Roots and Affixes |

Name: _____ Date: _____

Station One: Root Words

Root words are words from which many other words are formed. Root words can be used with a combination of roots and affixes.

Example: Word: *preview* Root Word: *view* Prefix: *pre-*
Example: Word: *removable* Root Word: *move* Prefix: *re-* Suffix: *-able*

Directions: Identify the root word for the following words.

Word **Root Word**

1. mountain _____
2. rescued _____
3. naturalist _____
4. stormy _____
5. loaner _____
6. kindness _____
7. answered _____
8. respectful _____
9. completed _____
10. misspell _____
11. migration _____
12. actor _____
13. champion _____
14. nervous _____
15. servant _____

Language Learning Stations — Roots and Affixes

Name: _____ Date: _____

Station Two: Adding Affixes

When you add an **affix** to a root word, you create a word with a new meaning. **Prefixes** are word parts added to the beginning of a word. **Suffixes** are word parts added to the end of a word.

Directions: Break down the following words into their word parts. Then write the meaning of the word. The first word is done for you. Use the Prefixes and Suffixes and the Greek and Latin Roots handouts if you need help.

Word	Prefix	Root/Base Word	Suffix	Meaning
1. unthinkable	un-	think	-able	not able to be thought of
2. autobiography				
3. cheerful				
4. multitask				
5. subzero				
6. semicircle				
7. slowly				
8. unresponsive				
9. bicycle				
10. closeness				

Station Three: Root Words, Affixes, and Context Clues

Directions: Read the excerpts from the classic story *Pollyanna* by Eleanor H. Porter. Break down the bold words into word parts. Then use context clues to write the meaning of the word as it is used in the excerpt.

Word	Prefix	Root/Base Word	Suffix	Meaning
1. disagreeable	dis-	agree	-able	not agreeable; unpleasant
2. undergarments				
3. pitifully				
4. unattractive				
5. incredulous				
6. happily				
7. sleepless				
8. refractory				
9. fluffiness				
10. uninterrupted				
11. pleasant				
12. sensation				
13. unable				
14. confident				
15. ungrateful				

LANGUAGE LEARNING STATIONS

Roots and Affixes

Name: _____ Date: _____

Station Four: Plural Forms of Latin Nouns

Example: Latin nouns ending in:
- **-a** change to **-ae** Example: *antenna* changes to *antennae*
- **-is** change to **-es** Example: *thesis* changes to *theses*
- **-us** change to **-i** Example: *stimulus* changes to *stimuli*
- **-um** change to **-a** Example: *medium* changes to *media*

Directions: Write the plural forms of the Latin nouns.

1. alumna _____
2. analysis _____
3. synopsis _____
4. cactus _____
5. crisis _____
6. cranium _____
7. curriculum _____
8. datum _____
9. focus _____
10. formula _____
11. fungus _____
12. larva _____
13. nucleus _____
14. referendum _____
15. syllabus _____

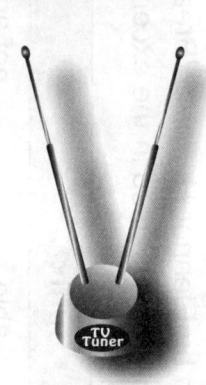

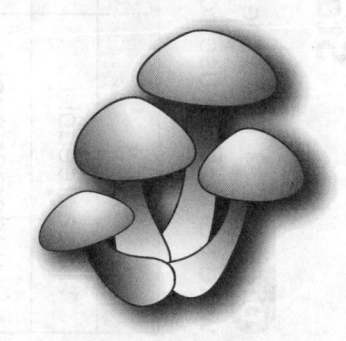

CD-404179 ©Mark Twain Media, Inc., Publishers

Prefixes and Suffixes

A prefix or suffix added to a root word makes a new word with a new meaning.

A **prefix** is a word part added to the beginning of a root word.

A **suffix** is a word part added to the end of a root word.

Prefix	Meaning
anti-	against
auto-	self
bi-	two
co-, com-, con-	together, with
de-	down, away, remove
dif-, dis-	not, opposite to
ex-	out, former
en-	put in
epi-	at, upon
fore-	before
hemi-	half
il-, im-, in-, ir-	not
inter-	between, among
mal-	bad
micro-	small
mid-	middle
mis-	not, wrong
mono-	one
multi-	many, much
non-	not
ob-, of-, op-	against
pre-	before
pro-	for
post-	after
quad-	four
re-	again, back
semi-	half
sub-	under, below
super-	above, over
tele-	distant, far off
trans-	across, beyond
tri-	three
un-	not, opposite of
under-	below, beneath
uni-	one
up-	above, higher

Suffix	Meaning
-able/-ible	capable of
-age	act of, state of being
-al	act of, like, of, pertaining to
-ance	act of, state of, quality of
-ant	having the quality of, one skilled in, one who
-ary	like, of, pertaining to
-ate	to make, quality of, state of
-en	to make
-ence	state of, quality of
-ent	being, one who
-er, -or	one who
-ess	one who (female)
-et, -ette	little, small
-ful	full of
-ian	person who
-ic	like, of, pertaining to
-ion, -ation	state or act of
-ish	like
-ism	like, of, state or quality of being
-ist	one who
-ity	being, state of
-ive	able to, having power to
-ly	like, manner of
-ize, -yze	to make into; to become
-less	without
-ment	act of, state, or quality of being
-ness	state of, a quality
-ous	full of, having
-some	full of, like
-ure	act of, state
-y	having the quality of, like

Greek and Latin Roots

The **root** is the part of a word that contains its basic meaning. Many roots cannot stand alone and are combined with affixes to form a word. Greek and Latin give English its most common roots. Knowing some of these word roots can help you decode many complex English words.

Root	Origin	Meaning	Example
aud	Latin	hear	auditorium, audible, audition
aut, auto,	Greek	self	autograph, autobiography
bell, belli	Latin	war	belligerent, bellicose, rebel
bio	Greek	life	biology, biome, biosphere
bibl, biblio	Greek	book	bibliography, bibliomania
cede	Latin	to go, yield	precede, recede, secede
chron, chrono	Greek	time	chronology, synchronize
cracy, crat	Greek	rule, govern	aristocrat, democracy
cred	Latin	believe, trust	credit, incredible, creditor
cycl	Greek	circle, wheel	bicycle, tricycle, recycle
dem	Greek	people	democracy, epidemic
derm	Greek	skin	dermatologist, taxidermy
dict	Greek	speak	contradict, predict
duc, duct	Latin	lead	conduct, deduction
fid	Latin	faith, trust	confidante, confidence
fort	Latin	chance, luck, strong	fort, fortress, fortunate
fract, frag	Latin	break	fracture, fragile, refractory
geo	Greek	earth	geology, geography
graph	Greek	write, record, draw	autograph, graphic
grat	Latin	pleasing, thankful	congratulate, gratuity
ject	Latin	to throw	project, deject, inject
manu	Latin	hand	manual, manufacture
meter, metr	Greek	measure	thermometer, barometer
migr	Latin	to move, wander	migration, immigrant
ortho	Greek	straight	orthodontist, orthodox
path	Greek	feeling, suffering	apathy, sympathy
ped	Latin	foot	pedicure, pedometer
phon	Greek	sound	microphone, phonograph
phot, photo	Greek	light	photosynthesis, photograph
port	Latin	carry	transport, import
rupt	Latin	break	rupture, abrupt, corrupt
scop, scope	Greek	see	microscope, telescope
scrib, script	Latin	write	subscribe, prescribe
sens, senti	Latin	feel	sentiment, sensation, sense
spec, spect	Latin	look, view, see	spectacle, spectator
sum	Latin	take, use, waste	consume, assume, presume
struct	Latin	build	construct, destruction
therm	Greek	heat	thermometer, thermos
topo	Greek	place	topography, topographical
vers, vert	Latin	turn	revert, diversion
vid, vis	Latin	see	video, visual
viv	Latin	life	revive, survive, survival

Pollyanna

Pollyanna by Eleanor H. Porter is the story of an orphaned girl sent to live with her aunt.

1. With a frown Miss Polly folded the letter and tucked it into its envelope. She had answered it the day before, and she had said she would take the child, of course. She HOPED she knew her duty well enough for that!—**disagreeable** as the task would be.

2. Nancy's capable hands made short work of unpacking the books, the patched **undergarments**, and the few **pitifully unattractive** dresses.

3. Pollyanna still looked **incredulous**, and with another long breath Nancy **happily** settled herself to tell the story.

4. Just how long she lay in **sleepless** misery, tossing from side to side of the hot little cot, she did not know; but it seemed to her that it must have been hours before she finally slipped out of bed, felt her way across the room and opened her door.

5. For five minutes Pollyanna worked swiftly, deftly combing a **refractory** curl into **fluffiness**, perking up a drooping ruffle at the neck, or shaking a pillow into plumpness so that the head might have a better pose.

6. During the whole process of getting started, the little girl had kept up an **uninterrupted** stream of comments and questions, until the somewhat dazed Nancy found herself quite out of breath trying to keep up with her.

7. She walked, indeed, two or three times back and forth from end to end—it gave her such a **pleasant sensation** of airy space after her hot little room...

8. "Anyhow, if they were up here, I just reckon they'd change and take Jimmy Bean for their little boy, all right," she finished, secure in her conviction, but **unable** to give a reason for it, even to herself.

9. Quietly, but with **confident** courage, Pollyanna ascended the chapel steps, pushed open the door and entered the vestibule.

10. "Oh, Aunt Polly, as if I ever could be **ungrateful**—to YOU! Why, I LOVE YOU—and you aren't even a Ladies' Aider; you're an aunt!"

(Excerpted from *Pollyanna* by Eleanor H. Porter)

LANGUAGE LEARNING STATIONS   Figurative Language

Teacher Page

Unit: Figurative Language

Goal: Students will demonstrate an understanding of figurative language.

Common Core State Standards (CCSS):

6th Grade	7th Grade	8th Grade
L.6.5. Demonstrate understanding of figurative language, word relationships, and nuances in word meanings. a. Interpret figures of speech (e.g., personification) in context. c. Distinguish among the connotations (associations) of words with similar denotations (definitions) (e.g., stingy, scrimping, economical, unwasteful, thrifty).	L.7.5. Demonstrate understanding of figurative language, word relationships, and nuances in word meanings. a. Interpret figures of speech (e.g., literary, biblical, and mythological allusions) in context. c. Distinguish among the connotations (associations) of words with similar denotations (definitions) (e.g., refined, respectful, polite, diplomatic, condescending).	L.8.5. Demonstrate understanding of figurative language, word relationships, and nuances in word meanings. a. Interpret figures of speech (e.g. verbal irony, puns) in context. c. Distinguish among the connotations (associations) of words with similar denotations (definitions) (e.g., bullheaded, willful, firm, persistent, resolute).

© Copyright 2010. National Governors Association Center for Best Practices and Council of Chief State School Officers. All rights reserved.

Materials List/Setup

Station 1: Alliteration (Activity)
Station 2: Metaphors in Newspapers (Activity); newspapers
Station 3: Figurative Language in Advertisements (Activity); Figures of Speech (Handout); magazines
Station 4: Idioms (Activity)

Activity: one copy per student
Handout: one copy per each student in a group

*Integration of Speaking and Listening Standards

Opening Activity and Discussion Questions (Teacher-Directed)

1. What is figurative language?
2. Can you name an example of figurative language?

Student Instructions for Learning Stations

At the learning stations, you will explore the different types of figurative language used by authors. Discuss your answers with other team members after completing each activity.

Closure: Reflection

The following questions can be used to stimulate discussion or as a journaling activity.
1. Why do you think people use figurative language when speaking and writing?
2. How does figurative language make fiction more interesting?

Language Learning Stations | Figurative Language

Name: _____ Date: _____

Station One: Alliteration

Alliteration is the use of the same consonant sound at the beginning of words that are near each other. The use of alliteration in tongue twisters can make the twister difficult to recite.

> **Example 1:** Famous letter "S/Sh" tongue twister
> *She sells seashells by the seashore.*
>
> **Example 2:** Famous letter "P" tongue twister.
> *Peter Piper picked a peck of pickled peppers.*
> *How many pecks of pickled peppers did Peter Piper pick?*

Directions: Use alliteration to write your own tongue twister. Share your tongue twister with your group. Practice saying the tongue twisters of other group members.

Step 1: Select a letter of the alphabet. Under the appropriate heading (nouns, proper nouns, verbs, and descriptive words) list words that begin with the letter you have selected.

Nouns	Proper Nouns	Verbs	Descriptive Words (adjectives & adverbs)

Step 2: Use the words above to write a tongue twister. Does your tongue twister make sense?

_____

_____

_____

Language Learning Stations Figurative Language

Name: _____ Date: _____

Station Two: Metaphors in Newspapers

A **metaphor** compares two unlike objects or ideas without using the words *like* or *as*. A metaphor states that something **is** something else.

Example: America is a melting pot.
first thing **is** a *second thing*

Directions: Select a newspaper from the station. Divide the sections of the newspaper among group members. For five minutes, each team member highlights as many metaphors as can be found in his or her section. Share findings with other team members.

1. Which section of the newspaper had the most metaphors? _____

2. Select three of the metaphors from the group's findings and complete the chart below

Metaphor	What is the figurative meaning of the metaphor?	Descriptive Words (adjectives and adverbs)

Language Learning Stations Figurative Language

Name: _____ Date: _____

Station Three: Figurative Language in Advertisements

Directions: Figurative language is used frequently in advertisements. Cut out four advertisements from magazines that use figurative language. Fill in the chart for each advertisement. Use the Figurative Language handout to help you. Staple the advertisements to the back of this paper.

Ad	Product Name	Figure of Speech	Figurative Language Wording From the Advertisement
1			
2			
3			
4			

Name: _____ Date: _____

LANGUAGE LEARNING STATIONS — Figurative Language

Station Four: Idioms

Directions: An **idiom** is an expression that says one thing but means something else. Choose two idioms from the list below. Using the example as a guide, complete the chart.

Give me a hand.
You're pulling my leg.
Zip your lips.
Don't bite off more than you can chew.
He had an ax to grind.
The cake is as light as a feather.
He is between a rock and a hard place.
Keep your eye on the ball.
Cat got your tongue?
She is in the doghouse.
He is all thumbs.
It cost me an arm and a leg.
He is barking up the wrong tree.
He is on pins and needles.

Idiom	Meaning	Illustration
Example: It is raining cats and dogs.	It is raining very hard.	
Idiom 1:		
Idiom 2:		

Create an idiom and write it on the lines below.

_____

_____

Figures of Speech

Figures of speech are literary devices. When used effectively, figures of speech bring a whole new meaning to written and spoken language. Below are some common types of figures of speech.

Figure of Speech	Definition	Example
Alliteration	repetition of the initial consonant sounds	Cal the cat caught a cold.
Hyperbole	statement that is deliberately exaggerated for effect	He threw the ball a mile.
Idiom	expression that says one thing but means something else	It is raining cats and dogs.
Irony	words or phrases that mean the opposite of the intended meaning	You ought to sleep well. You lie so easily!
Metaphor	direct comparison of two different things without using the words *like* or *as*	Rick is a bear this morning.
Onomatopoeia	word that sounds like its meaning	*Quack, quack* went the ducks.
Personification	giving human characteristics to an animal, non-living object, or an idea	The rustling leaves sang a song.
Pun	similar sounding words that create a humorous effect, better known as a "play on words."	Every time I get on a ferry boat it makes me cross.
Simile	comparison of two different things using the words *like* or *as*	Mary is as independent as a cat.

LANGUAGE LEARNING STATIONS   Vocabulary and Word Choice

Teacher Page

Unit: Vocabulary and Word Choice

Goal: Students will be able identify the connotation of words and the impact of the word choice.

Common Core State Standards (CCSS):

6th Grade	7th Grade	8th Grade
L.6.6. Acquire and use accurately grade-appropriate general academic and domain-specific words and phrases; gather vocabulary knowledge when considering a word or phrase important to comprehension or expression.	L.7.6. Acquire and use accurately grade-appropriate general academic and domain-specific words and phrases; gather vocabulary knowledge when considering a word or phrase important to comprehension or expression.	L.8.6. Acquire and use accurately grade-appropriate general academic and domain-specific words and phrases; gather vocabulary knowledge when considering a word or phrase important to comprehension or expression.

© Copyright 2010. National Governors Association Center for Best Practices and Council of Chief State School Officers. All rights reserved.

Materials List/Setup

Station 1: Mood (Activity)
Station 2: Word Choice (Activity); newspaper editorials; dictionaries (print or online); thesauruses
Station 3: Connotations: Positive, Negative, or Neutral (Activity)
Station 4: Vocabulary (Activity); The Star-Spangled Banner (Handout); dictionaries (print or online)

Activity: one copy per student
Handout: one copy per each student in a group

*Integration of Technology Skills

Opening Activity and Discussion Questions (Teacher-Directed)

1. What is the difference between tone and mood?
2. What is the difference between connotation and denotation?
3. What is a synonym?

Student Instructions for Learning Stations

At the learning stations, you will identify the connotation of words and analyze the impact the word choice has on the reader. Discuss your answers with other team members after completing each activity.

Closure: Reflection

The following question can be used to stimulate discussion or as a journaling activity.
1. Why is it important to consider both the denotation and connotation of words as you speak and write?

Language Learning Stations · Vocabulary and Word Choice

Name: _____ Date: _____

Station One: Mood

Mood is the feelings the reader gets from reading the author's words. Words have a positive or negative **connotation**, or feeling associated with them, in addition to their actual meaning.

Words That Can Be Used to Describe Mood

angry	gloomy	lonely	sorrowful
anxious	happy	mysterious	suspenseful
depressing	haunting	romantic	suspicious
excited	irritated	sad	tense
frightening	jealous	serious	uncomfortable
frustrating	joyful	sentimental	

Directions: Read the following paragraph and answer the questions below.

> Night came on, and a full moon rose high over the trees into the sky, lighting the land till it lay bathed in ghostly day. And with the coming of the night, brooding and mourning by the pool, Buck became alive to a stirring of the new life in the forest other than that which the Yeehats had made. He stood up, listening and scenting. From far away drifted a faint, sharp yelp, followed by a chorus of similar sharp yelps. As the moments passed the yelps grew closer and louder. Again Buck knew them as things heard in that other world which persisted in his memory. He walked to the center of the open space and listened. It was the call, the many-noted call, sounding more luringly and compellingly than ever before. And as never before, he was ready to obey. John Thornton was dead. The last tie was broken. Man and the claims of man no longer bound him.
>
> (Excerpt from *The Call of the Wild* by Jack London)

1. What is the mood of the paragraph? _____
   _____
   _____

2. What words helped you determine the mood? _____
   _____
   _____

3. Did the words have a positive or negative connotation? Explain your answer.
   _____
   _____

Language Learning Stations Vocabulary and Word Choice

Name: _____ Date: _____

Station Two: Word Choice

Authors choose words with a positive or negative connotation in order to influence the way a reader thinks or feels.

Example (positive connotation): The coach was firm about the amount of time spent doing drill exercises.

Example (negative connotation): The coach was unyielding about the amount of time spent doing drill exercises.

Directions: Select a newspaper editorial. Read the editorial and look for words that have a positive or negative connotation. Complete the chart below. An example is provided in the chart. Use a dictionary or thesaurus if you need help.

Word	Connotation: Positive or Negative	Synonyms With the Same Connotation
unyielding	negative	demanding, strict

CD-404179 ©Mark Twain Media, Inc., Publishers

Language Learning Stations — Vocabulary and Word Choice

Name: _____ Date: _____

Station Three: Connotations: Positive, Negative, or Neutral

Directions: The words in each word group have the same denotation (meaning) but have either a positive, negative, or neutral connotation (feeling associated with a word). Determine the connotation for each word in a word group and write the word under the appropriate column. Remember, the connotation of a word may vary from person to person. An example has been provided.

Word Groups	Positive	Negative	Neutral
skinny, thin, malnourished, scrawny, slender	slender	skinny, malnourished, scrawny	thin
scurry, run, dash, scamper, dart			
scary, frightening, creepy, sinister, disturbing			
sick, ill, unwell, under the weather, ailing			
fussy, demanding, hard to please, selective, particular			
mature, old, adult, grown-up, elderly			
house, home, abode, dwelling, shack			
composed, tranquil stress-free, restful			
joyful, glad, happy, cheerful			

CD-404179 ©Mark Twain Media, Inc., Publishers

Language Learning Stations — Vocabulary and Word Choice

Name: _____ Date: _____

Station Four: Vocabulary

Directions: Choose three unfamiliar words from the poem "The Star-Spangled Banner." Complete a graphic organizer for each word.

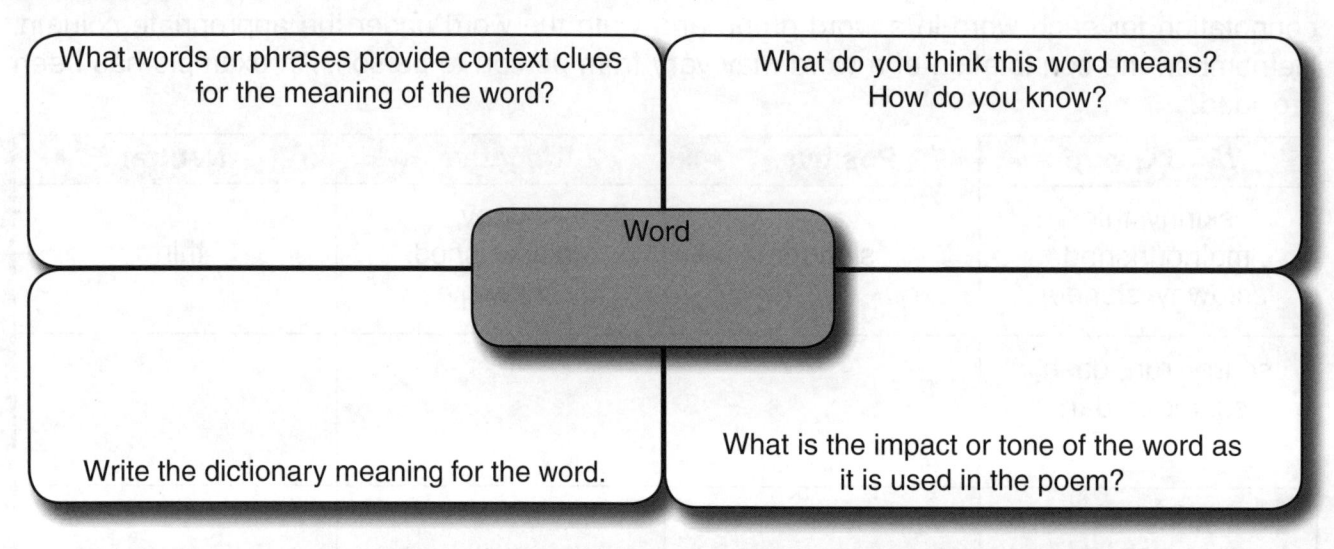

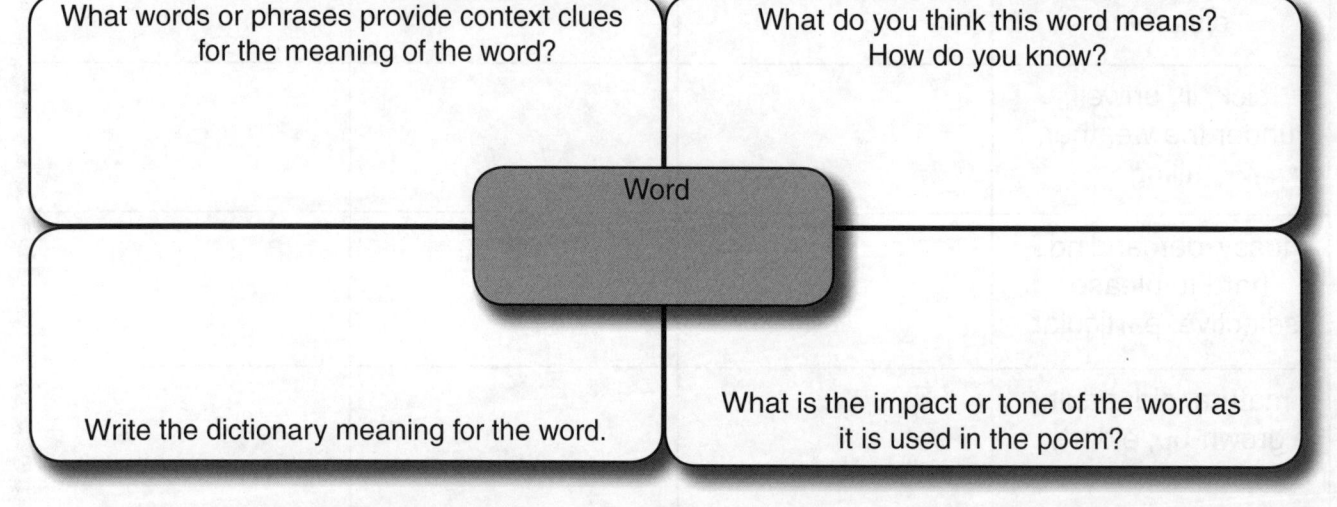

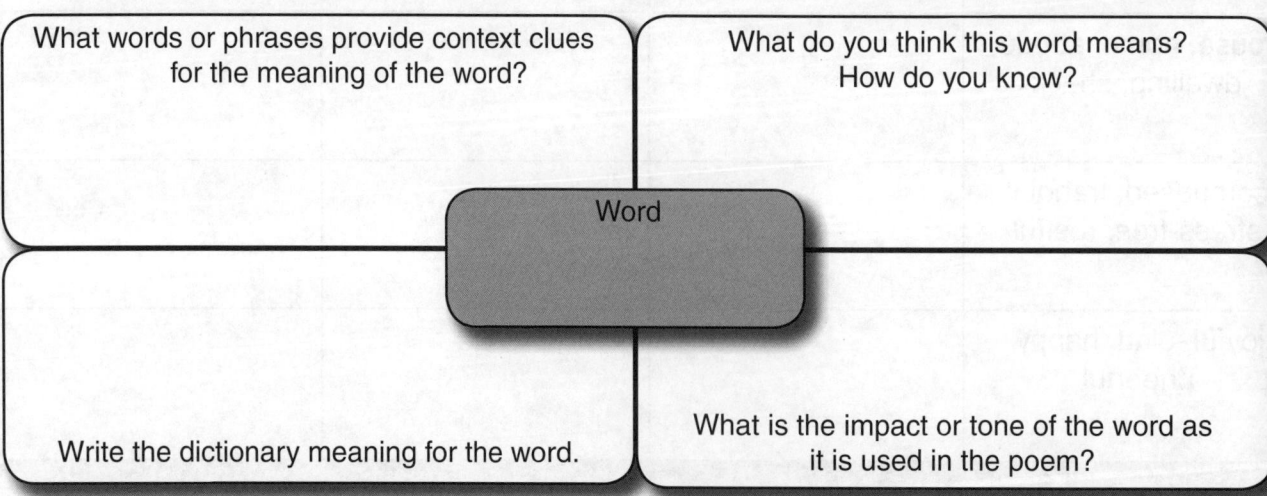

What words or phrases provide context clues for the meaning of the word?

What do you think this word means? How do you know?

Word

Write the dictionary meaning for the word.

What is the impact or tone of the word as it is used in the poem?

What words or phrases provide context clues for the meaning of the word?

What do you think this word means? How do you know?

Word

Write the dictionary meaning for the word.

What is the impact or tone of the word as it is used in the poem?

What words or phrases provide context clues for the meaning of the word?

What do you think this word means? How do you know?

Word

Write the dictionary meaning for the word.

What is the impact or tone of the word as it is used in the poem?

| Language Learning Stations | Vocabulary and Word Choice |

The Star-Spangled Banner

Francis Scott Key wrote his famous four-versed poem on September 14, 1814, during the Battle of Fort McHenry. The poem was later set to music. On March 3, 1931, the song officially became the national anthem.

The Star-Spangled Banner

O say, can you see, by the dawn's early light,
What so proudly we hailed at the twilight's last gleaming?
Whose broad stripes and bright stars, through the perilous fight,
O'er the ramparts we watched, were so gallantly streaming!
And the rockets' red glare, the bombs bursting in air,
Gave proof through the night that our flag was still there:
O say, does that star-spangled banner yet wave
O'er the land of the free and the home of the brave?

On the shore, dimly seen through the mists of the deep,
Where the foe's haughty host in dread silence reposes,
What is that which the breeze, o'er the towering steep,
As it fitfully blows, now conceals, now discloses?
Now it catches the gleam of the morning's first beam,
In full glory reflected now shines in the stream:
'Tis the star-spangled banner! O long may it wave
O'er the land of the free and the home of the brave!

And where is that band who so vauntingly swore
That the havoc of war and the battle's confusion
A home and a country should leave us no more?
Their blood has washed out their foul footsteps' pollution.
No refuge could save the hireling and slave
From the terror of flight, or the gloom of the grave:
And the star-spangled banner in triumph doth wave,
O'er the land of the free and the home of the brave!

Oh! thus be it ever, when freemen shall stand
Between their loved homes and the war's desolation!
Blest with victory and peace, may the Heaven-rescued land
Praise the Power that hath made and preserved us a nation.
Then conquer we must, for our cause it is just,
And this be our motto: "In God is our trust."
And the star-spangled banner in triumph shall wave
O'er the land of the free and the home of the brave!

Answer Keys

*If applicable, answers are provided.

Unit: Punctuation Usage
The Comma: Nonrestrictive Elements (pg. 4)
1. Rhode Island, the smallest state in land area, is a great place to go on vacation.
2. The rose bush in the front yard, which I planted, needs to be trimmed.
3. The Washington Monument, built between 1848 and 1884, was damaged by an earthquake.
4. The candidate, who has a degree in speech communication, was able to keep his speech under the thirty-minute time limit.
5. Mr. Jones, who likes to play golf, is a candidate for mayor.
6. My youngest brother, who lives in Oregon, helped me design a Website for my company.
7. Teresa, the friendliest girl in our class, was elected student body president.
8. The *Mona Lisa*, painted by Leonardo da Vinci, hangs in the Louvre Museum.
9. Michael, the oldest child in our family, was named after our uncle.
10. John Philip Sousa, an American composer, was famous for his patriotic marches.

The Dash (pg. 5)
1. c
2. c
3. a
4. d
5. b
6. c
7. a
8. c
9. d
10. c

Parentheses (pg. 6)
1. Green lizards (which were very rare in Puddleby) sat up on the stones in the sunlight and blinked at us.
2. After swooping over the sea around me (just looking for food, I supposed), he went off in the direction from which he had come.
3. I and my sister, Clippa (she was my favorite sister), had a very narrow escape for our lives.
4. He kept getting out his sextant (an instrument which tells you what part of the ocean you are in) and making calculations.
5. "The Sea!" murmured poor Clippa with a faraway look in her eyes (she had fine eyes, had my sister, Clippa).

Coordinate Adjectives (pg. 7)
1. light, fluffy
2. long, tedious
3. No coordinate adjectives
4. mouth-watering, delicious
5. narrow, winding
6. juicy, ripe
7. No coordinate adjectives
8. flaky, moist
9. long, grueling football (no comma between grueling and football)
10. slippery, wet

Unit: Spelling Conventions
Using Spelling Rules (pg. 9)
1. conscience: Write **i** before **e** when the vowel sound is **long e** except after **c**; The spelling **ce** is used for words with a long vowel sound followed by the ending **s** sound.
2. accelerator: There are lots of words which end in the **er** sound. It can be spelled **er**, **or**, and **ar**. Most of the words end with the **er** spelling.
3. acquire: **Q** is almost always followed by **u**.
4. torpedoes: Add **es** to most words that end in the letter **o**.
5. weight: Write **e** before **i** when the vowel sound is long **a**.
6. unnecessary: Adding a prefix never changes the spelling of a word.
7. shameful: In most cases, words ending in silent **e** keep the **e** if the suffix begins with a consonant (**-ly**, **-ful**, **-less**).

Language Learning Stations — Answer Keys

8. referring: Double the final consonant if the word has one syllable or the suffix begins with a vowel (**-ing**, **-ed**).
9. elves: Change the **f** or **fe** to **v** and add **es**.
10. suppression: Use **ion** or **sion** when the root word ends in **s** or **d**.

Syllables (pg. 12)
Syllabication may vary in different dictionaries.
1. rev/o/lu/tion
2. cap/i/tal
3. ban/dit
4. man
5. rub/ber
6. dec/la/ra/tion
7. pen/cil
8. pre/am/ble
9. un/sus/pect/ed
10. im/por/tant
11. e/lect
12. ath/lete
13. twi/light
14. um/pire
15. pad/dle
16. va/cant
17. blank
18. cal/cu/late
19. tem/per
20. chip

Unit: Reference Materials
Syllabication (pg. 18)
Syllabication may vary in different dictionaries.
1. hall/way (3)
2. des/sert (1)
3. ea/ger (2)
4. key/board (3)
5. pin/na/cle (1, 5)
6. pro/gram (4)
7. quick/ly (4)
8. re/spon/si/ble (1, 4, 5)
9. re/pel (2)
10. stark/ness (4)

Pronunciation of a Word (pg. 19)
1. lodge
2. quilt
3. horror
4. telephone
5. collection
6. origin
7. conduct
8. browse
9. swallow
10. nature
11. panic
12. habit
13. literature
14. acre
15. college

Unit: Roots and Affixes
Root Words (pg. 25)
1. mount
2. rescue
3. nature
4. storm
5. loan
6. kind
7. answer
8. respect
9. complete
10. spell
11. migrate
12. act
13. champion
14. nerve
15. serve

Adding Affixes (pg. 26)
Meanings will vary. Possible answers are given.

	Prefix	Root	Suffix
2.	auto-	bio, graph	-y

Meaning: writing about oneself

3.		cheer	-ful

Meaning: full of cheer; happy

4.	multi-	task	

Meaning: doing many tasks at once

Language Learning Stations — Answer Keys

5. sub- zero
   Meaning: below zero
6. semi- circle
   Meaning: half of a circle
7. slow -ly
   Meaning: in a slow manner
8. un-, re- spons -ive
   Meaning: not giving a response
9. bi- cycle
   Meaning: two wheels
10. close -ness
    Meaning: the quality of being close

Root Words, Affixes, and Context Clues (pg. 27)

Meanings will vary. Possible answers are given.

Prefix	Root/Base	Suffix

2. under- garment -s
   Meaning: clothes worn under other clothes
3. pity (i) -ful, -ly
   Meaning: in a manner deserving pity
4. un- attract -ive
   Meaning: not pretty
5. in- cred (ul) -ous
   Meaning: not able to believe
6. happy (i) -ly
   Meaning: in a happy manner
7. sleep -less
   Meaning: without sleep
8. re- fract -ory
   Meaning: resisting control; unmanageable
9. fluffy (i) -ness
   Meaning: quality of being fluffy
10. un-, inter- rupt -ed
    Meaning: unbroken; nonstop
11. please -ant
    Meaning: in a pleasing manner; agreeable
12. sens (e) -ation
    Meaning: a feeling or awareness

13. un- able
    Meaning: not able
14. con- fid -ent
    Meaning: certain; self-reliant
15. un- grate -ful
    Meaning: not grateful; not thankful

Plural Forms of Latin Nouns (pg. 28)

1. alumnae
2. analyses
3. synopses
4. cacti
5. crises
6. crania
7. curricula
8. data
9. foci
10. formulae
11. fungi
12. larvae
13. nuclei
14. referenda
15. syllabi

Unit: Figurative Language

The activities for this unit will require teacher verification.

Unit: Vocabulary and Word Choice

The activities for this unit will require teacher verification.